NEW YORK

A BOOK OF 21 POSTCARDS

BROWNTROUT PUBLISHERS
SAN FRANCISCO • CALIFORNIA

BROWNTROUT PUBLISHERS

P. O. BOX 280070 • SAN FRANCISCO • CALIFORNIA 94128-0070
800 777 7812 • www.browntrout.com

ISBN: 1-56313-847-6

BROWNTROUT publishes a large line of calendars, photographic books, and postcard books.
Please write for more information.

Printed in the U.S.A. by Chess Press
4977D Allison Parkway •Vacaville, California 95688 • 800 950 7812 • www.chesspress.com

NEW YORK

Early morning on Heart Lake, Adirondack Park and Preserve

PUBLISHED BY BROWNTROUT • SAN FRANCISCO, CALIFORNIA

NEW YORK

Marble columns of the Vanderbilt Mansion and the Hudson River

PUBLISHED BY BROWNTROUT • SAN FRANCISCO, CALIFORNIA

NEW YORK

Fall-colored huckleberry in the Shawangunk Mountains,
Minnewaska State Park

PUBLISHED BY BROWNTROUT • SAN FRANCISCO, CALIFORNIA

NEW YORK

The Vanderbilt Mansion, Hudson Valley,
Vanderbilt National Historic Site

PUBLISHED BY BROWNTROUT • SAN FRANCISCO, CALIFORNIA

NEW YORK

Lake Minnewaska, Minnewaska State Park

PUBLISHED BY BROWNTROUT • SAN FRANCISCO, CALIFORNIA

NEW YORK

Ice on Willowmemoc Creek, Catskill Mountains Park and Preserve

PUBLISHED BY BROWNTROUT • SAN FRANCISCO, CALIFORNIA

NEW YORK

Lake Placid, Adirondack Mountains, Adirondack Park and Preserve

PUBLISHED BY BROWNTROUT • SAN FRANCISCO, CALIFORNIA

NEW YORK

Large-flowered and purple trillium, Finger Lakes Region

PUBLISHED BY BROWNTROUT • SAN FRANCISCO, CALIFORNIA

NEW YORK

Bear Mountain Bridge spans the Hudson River

PUBLISHED BY BROWNTROUT • SAN FRANCISCO, CALIFORNIA

NEW YORK

Cascading Creek, Finger Lakes Region

PUBLISHED BY BROWNTROUT • SAN FRANCISCO, CALIFORNIA

NEW YORK

Rime-iced grasses on the summit of Mount Marcy,
Adirondack Mountains, Adirondack Park and Preserve

PUBLISHED BY BROWNTROUT • SAN FRANCISCO, CALIFORNIA

NEW YORK

Dock pilings at sunset, Northwest Harbor, Long Island

PUBLISHED BY BROWNTROUT • SAN FRANCISCO, CALIFORNIA

NEW YORK

Lake George seen from Rogers Rock, Adirondack Park and Preserve

PUBLISHED BY BROWNTROUT • SAN FRANCISCO, CALIFORNIA

NEW YORK

Early morning in the Shawangunk Mountains, Minnewaska State Park

PUBLISHED BY BROWNTROUT • SAN FRANCISCO, CALIFORNIA

NEW YORK

The Narrows of Lake George seen from the Tongue Range,
Adirondack Park and Preserve

PUBLISHED BY BROWNTROUT • SAN FRANCISCO, CALIFORNIA

NEW YORK

Wooden dory at sunset, Long Island

PUBLISHED BY BROWNTROUT • SAN FRANCISCO, CALIFORNIA

NEW YORK

Dame's rocket, Wyoming County

PUBLISHED BY BROWNTROUT • SAN FRANCISCO, CALIFORNIA

NEW YORK

Grasses on Algonquin Peak, Adirondack Park and Preserve

PUBLISHED BY BROWNTROUT • SAN FRANCISCO, CALIFORNIA

NEW YORK

Maple and birch trees along the Opalescent River,
Adirondack Park and Preserve

PUBLISHED BY BROWNTROUT • SAN FRANCISCO, CALIFORNIA

NEW YORK

Sunset glow, Montauk Point Lighthouse, Long Island

PUBLISHED BY BROWNTROUT • SAN FRANCISCO, CALIFORNIA

NEW YORK

Falls on Stony Creek, Catskill Mountains Park and Preserve

PUBLISHED BY BROWNTROUT • SAN FRANCISCO, CALIFORNIA